Contents

INTRODUCTION
Winesmanship; wine snobs and how to deal with them; how to describe wine and how to enjoy it.   5

CHAPTER ONE – How To Start
You are the customer; how to get what you want from the Wine Trade.   8

CHAPTER TWO – How to Choose a Wine
The two main categories of wine; bottling and labelling; what wine with what food; how to choose wine in a restaurant and how to dominate a wine waiter.   10

CHAPTER THREE – How to Store and Serve Wine
Where and how to keep it and present it; a guide to glasses; what to have in your cellar.   13

CHAPTER FOUR – The Theory of Wine
The history, chemistry and ageing of wine; all about the vines and the harvest.   18

CHAPTER FIVE – French Wines Without Tears
How to eat and drink your way through France by car and Alka-Seltzer.   21

CHAPTER SIX – The Vineyards of France
Champagne, Alsace, Burgundy, Rhone and Provence, Bordeaux, Sauternes, Entre Deux Mers, St. Emilion, The Loire.   22

CHAPTER SEVEN – German Wine
History of German wines; qualities and types; classifications; grapes and harvest; vineyards of Germany.   41

CHAPTER EIGHT – Wines of Spain
Sherry, table wines, spirits and liqueurs.   46

CHAPTER NINE – Wines of Portugal
Port, table wines, other fortified wines.   49

CONTENTS (continued)

CHAPTER TEN – The Wines of Italy

Chianti, Asti Spumante, Barolo, Vermouth, Martini, Cinzano, Carpaho, Campari, Gancia, Punt E Mes, Valpolicella, Soave ... to name but a few. 51

CHAPTER ELEVEN – The Wines of the Rest of the World

Wines of Africa, the Americas, Australia, and the countries of Europe not already covered. 52

A TOTALLY USELESS GLOSSARY TO BLUFF PEOPLE WITH 55

KNOW YOUR VINTAGES – The Wine and Food Society Vintage chart 63

Illustrations by Rex Clifford

The bluffer's guides

BLUFF YOUR WAY IN
Wine

NICK CLARKE

Wolfe Publishing Ltd

10 Earlham Street London WC2

This tome is respectfully dedicated to the large lady who stampeded an entire herd of Old Etonian wine merchants by describing an inoffensive Moselle as being 'tender, without being mawkish.'

OTHER TITLES ALREADY PUBLISHED:

The Bluffer's Guide to Literature
The Bluffer's Guide to Finance
The Bluffer's Guide to Music
The Bluffer's Guide to the Theatre
The Bluffer's Guide to Marketing
The Bluffer's Guide to Art
The Bluffer's Guide to Social Climbing
The Bluffer's Guide to Folk and Jazz
The Bluffer's Guide to the Cinema
The Bluffer's Guide to Management
The Bluffer's Guide to Antiques
The Bluffer's Guide to Ballet
The Bluffer's Guide to Opera
The Bluffer's Guide to Teaching
The Bluffer's Guide to Advertising
The Bluffer's Guide to Accountancy

Coming Shortly:
The Bluffer's Guide to P.R.

SBN 72340017 2

© Wolfe Publishing Ltd 1967, Reprinted 1971

**Made and printed in Great Britain
by C. Nicholls & Company Ltd.**

Introduction

Winesmanship as a cult
IT MUST BE REMEMBERED that wine can give a lot of real pleasure, like getting into a hot bath, eating a delicious meal, making love or lying in the sun – and real pleasures should neither be misused nor rejected with Puritan horror.

But to love wine is a slightly esoteric pleasure involving a blend of the mind, the senses and the bank balance. Traditionally, such pleasures have tended to be the privilege of the leisured classes; which allows a genuine pleasure to be spoilt by very tiresome snobs.

Wine Snobs
The wine snob, like all other sorts of snob, has, poor chap, a crashing inferiority complex. He is so conscious of feeling inadequate within himself that he uses his real – or imagined – knowledge of wine to make his unfortunate acquaintances feel ignorant, on the principle that he will be bigger if they are made smaller. He has an image of himself as an aristocratic and sophisticated man of the world, well travelled and a brilliant conversationalist. He has to maintain this image of himself, even if it involves boring and humiliating everybody he knows.

Anti-Wine-Snob Techniques
Stephen Potter suggests we develop a vocabulary of boldly meaningless expressions such as describing a wine as having 'too many tramlines.' He refers us to the 'Odoreida technique'. After a pompous bit of wine talk, we can say: 'Well, let's have a real drink. Popskull they call it in Nevada. We mix two parts of vodka with one of sherry and three of rum, adding a slice cut from the disc of a sunflower.' We imply we know little about wine, but we also suggest that the wine snob could not last long in a country where men are men. A variation of this is to ask the other if he has ever drunk rice wine from a Japanese girl's navel.

Erudition, not bluffing
The ultimate defence against the wine snob is to be able to develop a knowledge of the subject, which will give one enough self confidence to be able to say 'come off it' without having to indulge in a boring bit of one-upmanship.

The Pleasure of Wine

The pleasure of wine lies in being able to develop the sense of smell and taste so distinctly as to be able to appreciate how beautiful certain wines are as a finished whole. The pleasure lies in developing an intellectual interest in how the wine is made and where it comes from – which can make a foreign holiday very enjoyable, if drunk-making. The pleasure lies in sharing one's enthusiasms with others – *but only if they are keen themselves.*

Description of Wine

It is easy to see how Thurberian language has crept in. It is very difficult to describe something which has undergone so many changes since it was simple grape juice. Hence words like big, soft, supple, elegant, fruity, fresh, flinty, etc. Perhaps the most sensible thing to do would be to, in the beginning, confine one's description to the obvious: red, white or rosé, French, German or Italian, burgundy or claret, sweet or dry. The point of the weirder words will become apparent with experience.

How to Enjoy Wine

It's an awful waste to swig wine down like beer. Wine has five separate areas of enjoyment which can't be appreciated if it's gulped.

BOUQUET OR SMELL

Wine should be poured into a large, clear glass (we'll talk about glasses later) halfway up. The base of the glass should be kept on the table and, holding it by the stem, should be steadily revolved. This process exposes the wine to the air, enabling it to release what can be a most gorgeous and satisfying smell. Bury your nose in the glass and try it out for yourself. It is like inhaling celestial Friars Balsam. The scents of good wine are almost indescribable in their subtlety. One can find the smell of blackcurrants in fine Chablis, the sea in Muscadet, greengages in Sancerre, flowers in Beaujolais and tannin in Claret. But everybody's ideas vary, and one should not be bluffed into accepting the subjective judgement of someone else.

THE APPEARANCE OF THE WINE

If you have any coloured wine glasses, it would be a very good idea if you gave a Russian party, and smashed them all. All wine glasses should be of clear glass if one is to enjoy the colours of wine. Negatively, it is important to be able to check that there is no sediment or bits of cork in the wine. Positively the colours can be a delight. The clarity and brilliance, the purple-red of Beaujolais, the deep brown-red of old Claret, the greenness or yellowness of white wines, the 'onion skin' edge of some rosés – if one is sensitive to colour, it is possible to obtain great pleasure from the sight of wine.

Now Comes the Tasting Itself
FORETASTE:
A sip of wine should be placed in the front of the mouth and considered with the tastebuds on the front of the tongue, and the inside part of the mouth.
MAIN TASTE
Air should be drawn into the mouth, and a gargling-like process will release many flavours in the mouth as a whole.
AFTER TASTE:
Finally, the wine is allowed to trickle down one's throat and over the back of the tongue. Then one can bask in the glorious afterglow of, one hopes, a perfectly balanced wine.

It is only after going through these five distinct processes that we can hope to draw any really accurate conclusion as to a wine's quality: let alone derive maximum enjoyment.

The Instant Connoisseur
A good palate for wines is developed by:
(a) Frequently going through the process described in the previous paragraph, while, intellectually:
(b) Taking the trouble to understand where the wine comes from, how it is made and from what grape: learning about its reported characteristics in relation to what one is tasting: and taking every advantage to cement this knowledge by tasting wine intelligently whenever one is abroad, or at a good tasting.
(c) If one effects a happy and enjoyable marriage of taste and mind as described, it becomes worthwhile to spend some money on what is a real pleasure. Far too many wine snobs do not appreciate what they are tasting: they buy expensive wine – frequently bogus – at ridiculous prices as a status symbol. If wine becomes a real pleasure, it might become worthwhile to allow one's taste buds and sense of smell to become more sensitive by refraining from smoking and drinking hard spirits on the rocks. You must choose between the real enjoyment of wine and the psychedelic properties of tobacco (LSD, come to that) and hard alcohol: that they won't mix must be recognised. The only time it is categorically wrong, on a good manners basis, to smoke, is while wine is being tasted and proper food is being eaten.

CHAPTER ONE

How to Start

YOU ARE the potential consumer of a product handled by a multi-million pound business. This business – the booze trade – is dying to make a sale. Never, ever, forget that you are in a privileged position. A good wine merchant – like a good anything else – is a man who has a deep love, knowledge and respect for his product. He will want your trade for life and will want to help, not by forcing you to buy an expensive wine for the sake of a quick sale, but, by interpreting intelligently your wishes and your needs. Then he can expect from you a permanent loyalty. You become an excellent long-term investment for him and his business. If he can't be bothered, go to someone who can.

The Wine Trade – General

The wine trade, in Britain, is becoming far too much the playground of enormous combines of brewers, distillers and big groups. Most of the chain off-licences and pubs are owned by a group of one sort or another. The disadvantage of this, for the consumer, is that a manager of an individual off-licence or pub will be pressurised into pressurising you into buying one of their proprietary blended wines. This sort of wine may be perfectly OK: It is unlikely to be really excellent, as quantity rather than quality has to be the buying policy of the big boys. It would be a very intelligent move, on the part of the big groups, to form wine clubs for their serious customers. They could have a special list of special wines for special customers. They could arrange tastings and courses of instruction in wines. They could offer these wines at wholesale prices, by the case of twelve bottles. Some do this already: genuine wine appreciation would spread if it became general. There are, however, some independent merchants who can do all this more easily. A small business can give a personal service denied to the chain store: wine must be intensely personal and a serious consumer is well-advised to discover if such a merchant can easily be contacted and to establish a personal entente with him.

The Structure of the Wine Trade

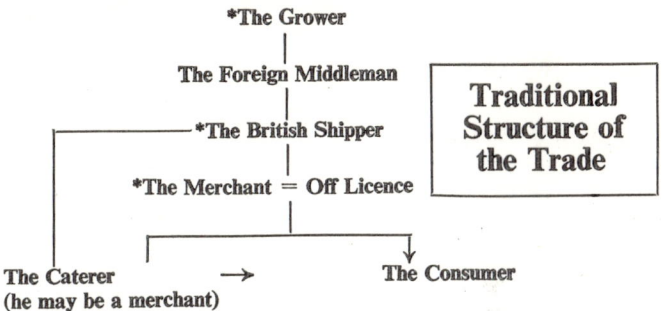

It can be seen, therefore, that such is the wish to sell wine, a consumer is mad if he does not buy wine by the case, and expect to receive good advice about what to choose. The only problem is that one tends to drink more if the stuff is available. But is this a disadvantage?

Finally, the reason for the building up of the big groups is money. Wine has to be bought and paid for long before any money is received. Credit has to be serviced: enormous sums of capital must be available. The wine trade is having to handle the wine from source to consumer in order to enjoy the maximum profit all along the line. Thus they can service the capital involved: but can they develop a personal service for the customer?

Private Wine Clubs

There are various private wine clubs run on a non-profitmaking cooperative basis as syndicates. Obviously this can mean cheaper prices, and a lot of fun by being in on tasting and buying. It is questionable, however, whether many growers would sell their finest wines to such limited markets. The answer, obviously, depends entirely on who runs

---

*Certain big groups own vineyards, ship their own wine themselves and market the wine to the public and to other merchants. Certain caterers have a wholesale licence enabling them to buy wine at 'shippers price'. They will (a) sell the wine at 'restaurant price' to customers by the bottle in the restaurant and (b) sell the wine at 'wholesale price' by the case for customers to drink at home.

the club – his ability to choose wine and pick good sources. The only criterion of this lies in judging – at a tasting – the overall quality in relation to price of the wines: and to do this, one needs some experience.

CHAPTER TWO
How to Choose a Wine

THERE ARE ONLY two sorts of wine worth bothering about, because in fact, there are only two sorts of occasion in most people's lives when wine is drunk.

(a) Either one is with chums and one wants to be able to get through quantities of perfectly acceptable inexpensive wine and have a party.
(b) The occasion is gastronomic, in which case appreciative company, and good food deserve fine wines.

It is vital to be honestly analytical of any one occasion, if it is to be a success and if money is not going to be wasted.

The Bottling Bit

Bearing this in mind, the two main categories of wine are:

LONDON BOTTLED WINES

Very acceptable wine can be found which has been imported into this country in cask and been bottled here. The shipper saves a lot of money on transport costs and the wine would not have cost him very much, anyway. He is able, therefore, to offer these wines at inexpensive prices. One of the best ways of judging the quality of a merchant is to taste his cheap, everyday, wine. Any fool can buy a good wine if money is no object: it is much cleverer to find really good cheap stuff.

ESTATE BOTTLED WINES

A grower who has any pride in his product will insist on bottling his finest wines himself. He will charge more for such wine, the cost of importation being greater, so they will cost the consumer more. But if the shipper can be trusted to buy wine from impeccable sources such wine is the very finest of its particular type. Does the occasion warrant the expense?

Apart from the implications of how a wine has been bottled, the choice must depend on the consumer knowing what a wine is and how much it should cost. An estate bottled wine from the Romanée Conti or a first growth claret is a much more important and rarer wine than, say, an estate bottled single vineyard Moulin à Vent. One might be six times as expensive as the other, but both, of their sort, are impeccable. Once again it becomes necessary to be objective about the ability of the company to appreciate the wine in relation to its cost.

Appellation Controllee

In France, they have very strict laws to control the labelling of wines. If an avaricious peasant were able to pour any old red wine into a bottle and to persuade an unsuspecting public that they were trying something special, he would be able to con them out of a lot of money. The appellation laws are designed to guarantee where the wine came from and, in the production, that the wine should be fairly representative of its reputation.

In England, however, the appellation laws do not apply. Gentlemen in Ipswich, apparently, have a habit of blending goodness knows what in great vats and calling it "Nuits St. Georges" or "Chateauneuf du Pape" or whatever may sound an attractive commercial name. This is the reason why it tends to be a waste of money to buy a London bottled wine with a well known name at a medium price: it is neither one thing or the other. The exception to this is claret: Bordeaux has such a defined and controlled structure, that a good London bottled bourgeois growth can be an excellent buy.

Labels on French Wines

A label should state the district where the wine is grown, and/or the vineyard or chateau. A label should proclaim the 'négociant' or shipper's name. A label should give the year of the harvest. A label should say if a wine is French or English bottled – 'Mise en bouteille and chateau,' 'au domaine' or 'dans mes caves' – or, alternatively, 'shipped by and bottled for XYZ of such and such an address'.

All this can be boiled down once again to reminding the consumer that he is at the mercy of the honesty or dishonesty of his merchant. A good merchant worthy of your custom will not sell you wine under false pretences.

What Wine With What Food

An awful lot of dreary snobbery is attached to this, quite unnecessarily. The ultimately correct choice is for the consumer to have exactly the wine he or she likes. Certain general guides are more or less common sense: and a consensus of other people's experience can help anyone who has to plan a menu for a special party.

Sherry is very acceptable with soup – which can often be jazzed up by pouring some into it.

Dry white wine is delicious with shellfish and whitefish, or as an aperitif.

Fuller white wine is delicious with freshwater fish, chicken, veal or pork.

Light red wine is delicious with simply roasted or grilled red meat or chicken.

Bigger red wine is delicious with game and strongly flavoured meat dishes.

Any red wine is delicious with cheese.

Sweet white wine is delicious with puddings or as an aperitif.

Rosé can be drunk as an aperitif – or with almost anything in the summer.

Champagne can be drunk with anything or at any time – especially at breakfast, with a pretty girl.

How to Choose Wine in a Restaurant

Price

All caterers should supply a reasonable range of wines in the two main categories: some customers want good everyday wine which is not too expensive, whereas others want something grand. Any catering establishment which fails to provide this service, does not deserve a clientele. If a caterer takes the trouble to obtain a wholesale wine licence, he can buy wine at 'shippers price' – which is the rock bottom price at which wine is obtainable out of bond in this country. He can continue to work on the same mark-up – unless he has a huge turnover it is very difficult to cover overheads at less than 100% – but it means that his customers have a fair deal in relation to the luxury of his establishment. A very little experience will tell the customer what he should be paying.

The Wine List

The wine list in a restaurant should tell the customer as much as possible about the wines. He may merely order a red carafe but he should be able to know:

(a) **Clarets:** The name of château, the district and the classification. The year, the bottling, half bottles or not, and price.

(b) **Burgundy:** The name of the district, the vineyard and the négociant. The year, the bottling, half bottles or not and price.

(c) **Other French wines:** the same – but for négociant, read grower.

(d) **German wines:** the full and complicated German name system, the year, the bottling, half bottles and price.

The same principles apply, obviously, to any other wines the restaurateur may list: it is a good way to interest his clientele if he 'makes a story' about something unusual. He should also be prepared to give the antecedent of his carafe wines: many don't.

How to Dominate a Wine Waiter

There are many ways of subduing a wine waiter whose manner seems to say, 'Yes, it is my table, but you are not my sort of people.' You can, of course, hit him or pour the wine over his head. But, if you are to enjoy your evening, the 'gastronomic inspector' approach is to be recommended. It is vital to be impassive and portentous in one's study of the wine list. You should say to your companion – quietly, but audibly – 'They wanted me to try their house wines' – then, to the waiter: 'Tell me about the wine you sell in carafes.' He will probably tell you that it is red, white or rose . . . 'Yes, I realise that, but where does it come from' or 'Who is the grower/négociant/shipper?' Then, very gently: 'May I see the manager?' When the manager appears: 'Would you be very kind and allow me to take a copy of the menu and wine list away with me – unless there are going to be any alterations in the near future?' If anyone has the nerve to ask you who you represent, you must reply – charmingly, of course, that you must remain anonymous. If the manager can be bluffed into pressing free hospitality on you, enjoy it. In defence of caterers, it must be emphasised that the Clement Freud approach should be reserved for defence against unprovoked aggression, like the hydrogen bomb.

CHAPTER THREE
How to Store and Serve Wine

WHILE THE STORAGE and service of wine will be dealt with as for a restaurant, the principles, obviously, apply in one's own house.

(i) Bulk wine deliveries should be unpacked and the bottles stored in a cellar, on their side at an even temperature of about 50°–55° F., away from the light. Provided this is done, most wine should keep perfectly for ages. Light, fresh, wines do not last as long as big ones – and one should become acquainted with what needs drinking – always assuming one's lack of thirst makes such knowledge necessary.

(ii) A caterer has to serve wine from a dispense bar of some kind. Obviously he must keep a supply of his fast-selling wine at the right temperature, but, unless his clientele is very expense account inclined, he is quite justified in not keeping his really expensive wine at temperatures which might enable them to deteriorate if they are not often asked for.

(iii) It is much easier, in the home, to allow the wines to come to the right temperature. Violent changes of heat are very harmful to the wine: gently simmering Chateau Latour, or an iced lolly of Le Montrachet should be avoided. White wines are perfect if kept in a fridge for half an hour (from cellar temperature). Red wines should be a few degrees above room temperature – which can be done with the cork removed. Young Beaujolais is delicious at cellar temperature.

(iv) Wine is presented to the host in a restaurant for four good reasons. It is the customer's duty to ensure that:
(a) The wine is what he asked for.
(b) The size of bottle is correct (as opposed to halves, for example).
(c) The vintage is correct.
(d) The temperature is right.

Only then should the customer authorise the wine waiter to open the bottle, and to go through the ceremony of sniffing and tasting the wine. It is considered very OK to judge the soundness of the wine on smell alone. If the customer fails to check the bottle before opening, or if he wishes to return the opened wine for any reason except that the particular bottle is 'off', the restaurateur has the right to refuse to carry the can. He need not feel responsible for the subjective likes and dislikes of his guests, nor need he allow them to ignore the implications of the wine waiter's original presentation.

(v) White wine is frequently served from the cellar in an ice bucket. If the wine in the neck of the bottle is not cold enough, turn the bottle upside down. There should be no sediment, so it won't come to any harm – provided the cork is not removed, of course.

(vi) Red wine can throw a deposit, in which case it is necessary to decant it. Decanting also allows oxygen to get to the wine, which enables it to 'breathe' – so it can never harm and frequently benefit any red wine to be decanted. Decanting should be done against a candle, which enables one to see through the neck of the bottle when one has reached any sediment. Remove, very gently, the wine from its rack and, very slowly stand it up. Take the cork out – preferably using a corkscrew which, on a counterscrew principle, makes physical strength unnecessary. Wipe the mouth and neck of the bottle and remove any foil. Hold a clean decanter by the base of its neck in the left hand. Hold the bottle by its body in the right hand and gently tilt it so the wine pours – slowly and steadily – into the decanter. The light of the candle through the neck of the bottle should enable one to see when any sediment is reached. If this process is done steadily enough, very little wine should be wasted.

Wine baskets are quite unnecessary and pretentious. If the wine is very 'hard' – has a lot of tannin in it – it may need some hours of exposure to the air before it can 'breathe' and become alive. If time does not allow this, you can pour the decanted wine into another decanter and back again – which process will speed up the whole operation. While decanting is always desirable, it is not, obviously, necessary for the enjoyment of young wines.

(vii) Finally, the cork should be examined to make sure it is not rotten and that, in the case of estate bottled wines, it is stamped with the grower's certificate of origin. A nude and virgin cork out of a bottle of fine wine can be suspicious.

Wine Glasses

A lot of chi-chi nonsense is talked about wine glasses. The ultimate requirements for a satisfactory wine glass is that it should be
(a) Big
(b) Watertight
(c) Clear
(d) On a stem.

Most of the nonsense about glasses stems from certain wine areas having traditional glasses. The ultimate abomination is the sort of saucer-like champagne glasses one gets at weddings – unless, of course, one likes still champagne.

What the Well-Dressed Cellar has in It

Above all else, obviously, booze, but a selection is almost entirely controlled by what one can afford. If we ignore spirits which will or will not be there – depending on how important they are in anyone's life – the wine cellar will consist of an everyday and a special list. The following suggestions are entirely subjective ones:

Everyday List

All these wines are from good merchants and have been bottled in England.
Red
  A French Vin de Consommation.
  A Young Genuine Beaujolais.
  A monopole claret.
  A good Spanish or Portuguese red (if this can be found).
  A strong wine from the Cotes du Rhone.

A NO-NONSENSE
GUIDE TO GLASSES

 *Sherry and chilled aperitifs, As big as they come*

 *Champagne & sparkling wines, still white wines, perhaps*

 *All table wines, 12oz Paris goblet*

 *Brandy and liqueurs, about the size of an orange*

 Scotch and gin, huge and heavy

White
　A Muscadet or Gros Plant from Nantes.
　A white Beaujolais or Macon.
　A Reisling from Alsace or South Germany.

Rose
　A Rose de Cabernet from Anjou.
　A dry Tavel or 'Pelure d'Oignon'.
　A good Portuguese Rose (if, again, this can be found).

Special List

Assuming we have a limited budget, we can forget first growth clarets and the great wines of the Côtes de Nuits. We are also, in view of the money involved, dependent on our merchant.

CLARET

Good Bourgeois and 3rd and 4th growth classified wines – both chateau and London bottled – can, with good advice, be found.

BURGUNDY

It is vital to buy wines which come from a respectable négociant. The softer wines from the Côtes de Beaune, the Côtes Challonais, and Maconnais are very good buys – both red and white.

CHAMPAGNE

One can buy 'grandes marques' champagnes quite successfully at auctions. BOB champagnes can be delicious, and most merchants can get inexpensive fizzy wine suitable for cocktails or Bucks Fizz.

LOIRE

An estate bottled Muscadet, a good Sancerre, Vouvray or a Pouilly Blanc Fumé.

APERITIFS AND DIGESTIVES

Sirop de Cassis is useful as you can make 'vin blanc cassis' in the summer. Vermouth de Chambéry is delicious, dry and slightly lemon flavoured, by itself or with gin. Some merchants are clever enough to find a 'pale fine brandy' which is pure and clean if not very old. Such brandy is often excellent value, selling at a price between three stars and VSOP. A good sherry – fino, preferably – is essential.

How to Know Your Stuff

A bluffer's guide is meant only as instant erudition. It is advisable therefore, for anyone who is seriously interested in learning about wine, to have seriously informative books on the subject. The following can be highly recommended:

The Wines and Vineyards of France by Louis Jacquelin and Rene Poulain.

The Wines of France by Alexis Lichuoe.

The Great Wines of Germany by Andre Smith and S. F. Hallgarten.

The Wines of Italy by Cyril Ray.

The danger is that the study of such books, plus the opportunity to partake in intelligent and regular tastings, can change a wine bluffer into a wine snob.

CHAPTER FOUR
The Theory of Wine
History of Wine

WINE IS AS OLD as civilisation itself. References are found among the records of Mesopotamia and Egypt, and, as any schoolboy who has had the doubtful privilege of a classical education will know, wine pervades the literature of Greece and Rome. The vine travelled from Babylon or Assyria to Egypt to Greece to Rome. The Romans, in the course of their empire building, brought it to France, Germany and Spain. In more recent history, the wine has travelled from Europe to America, Africa and Australia.

Historical allusions provide invaluable scope for the imaginative wine bluffer, being a particularly effective weapon against the wine snob: such allusions are difficult to disprove and are outside the usual context of personal reminiscenses and technical 'in-isms'. Since the most effective lies are those which stick closest to the truth, it is advisable for the earnest wine bluffer to brush up his history, concentrating particularly on the rich field of ancient mythology. Dionysus, The Maenads, Homer's wine-dark sea, Nausicaa, Silenus, Bacchus, the Nymphs and Satyrs, Astarte, Lucullus – such beautiful names can be mixed with a grand disregard for any actual mythological or historical accuracy. If anyone questions one's authenticity, it is always possible to put the blame on Horace, Petronius or Sappho, who can't answer back. 'It is such a wine as this that drove the wild-eyed Maenads to rend their clothes and tear poor Narcissus asunder under the pale glow of Astarte's light'. 'In this old claret, I fancy I can hear the rich chuckle of Silenus'. 'Oh for the pen of Horace to praise such Lucullan delights.' Provided a wine waiter is short, fat and rather unattractive, one can always ask him to 'play the Ganymede' just before he has got around to serving the wine. Classical allusions should be reserved for fulsome praise rather than informed criticism: if one had the knowledge, one would not need the classics, after all. The wine bluffer must practise a solemn, deadpan delivery of such bons mots: his aim is to be able to produce, at the drop of an allusion, a stunned, horrified silence.

The Vines Themselves

There is an enormous number of different varieties of vine, all of which will produce, obviously, different wines. Sometimes the vines are named on the label of the wine itself: Rose d'Anjou de *Cabernet*, Bourgogne *Aligote*, Reisling and Traminer are all names of different varieties.

A vine grown in different soils, with different climates and different methods of viticulture will, again, produce very different wines: the Sauvignon grape, for example, produces both Sauternes and Pouilly Blanc Fumé.

Vines grow between 28° and 50° of latitude, but the altitude will affect their success, especially in the northern areas. The greatest vineyards, often first planted by the Romans, are grown along the northern limits of the wine producing areas. The wines of Bordeaux, the Loire, Champagne, Burgundy, Alsace, and the Rheingau are produced in relatively colder climates than the more abundant areas of the South, and are much more delicate and subtle.

The Viticulture and the Harvest

Good grapes, must, obviously, be planted on soil which will produce good wine, and the vigneron must tend his vines with enormous care. Too much potassium, nitrogen, or organic manure will produce lush vegetation, but little fruit. Too much water will produce swollen and tasteless grapes. There is a perpetual fear of the wrong weather: too much fierce sun dries the pulp, too much rain produces only a minor crop, heat can destroy an entire harvest and a frost at the wrong time can stop a year's produce before it starts. Hence the jubilation at a 'good year'.

The harvest is gathered when the grapes are ripe: the natural acid decreases and the sugar increases. The colour of the grapes changes, a 'black' grape changes from green to red, and a 'white' grape turns from green to yellow. A naturally sweet wine, like Sauternes, has its grapes left on the vine until a mildewy rot – 'the pourriture noble' – has set in, which makes it particularly vulnerable to the elements.

The Vinification

Once the grapes have been picked and have been brought to the pressing cellar, the process of vinification begins. This is done in one of three ways: either the skins, pips and stems are left in with the juice to produce red wine, or the juice is separated from the pressings to produce white wine. A third method – a compromise between the two – produces a natural rosé. The vigneron, who will know what sort of wine he is going to produce will add yeast to the pressed grape juice, which converts the natural sugar into alcohol.

The Chemistry of Wine

Enormous chemical changes happen when yeast is added to the recently pressed grape juice.

Sugar + yeast = alcohol + carbonic acid gas.

The newly made wine, sitting in vast vats, needs constant supervision: the acidity, the alcohol level, the tannin content, the temperature, and flaws or dangers need counteracting and balancing. Science helps the vigneron to protect himself against natural hazards. The addition of sugar, citric acid, gum arabic, bentonite, sulphur, glycerine and Uncle Tom Cobbleigh and all can protect and preserve. The sugar/alcohol conversion is very energetic and the contents of the vat seethe for a few days – and the livelier the vat, the better the chance of a good wine. The use of the filter, the blending of different wines and different vintages, and the addition of more sugar are tricks of the trade which are tightly controlled by law in most wine producing countries. There is a lot of controversy about the use of science in the making of wine: the old school believes that what was good enough for father is good enough for them, while the mods point out that science can help the vigneron's bank balance, and, anyway, that we rely on medical science quickly enough when we get ill.

The Ageing of Wine

The wine is now put into casks and countless micro-organisms act upon its chemical structure and effect countless changes. It is alive, and, like all living things, must be allowed to reach full maturity if it is to produce its full strength and quality. The knowledge of when a wine is ready for drinking can never be assessed by computers: it comes from deep knowledge and deep love. The ageing of wine is in two stages.
(a) While the wine is in the vat it is in direct contact with the air and the oxygen enables it to lose some of its harshness and astringency.
(b) When the wine is sealed from the air in cask, or even more firmly, in bottle, the development is much slower, gradually enabling a great wine to show all the nuances of depth, bouquet, and smooth-

ness which go to give the harmonious pleasure for which it can be considered worth paying high prices.

This is, of course, one of the main reasons why great wine – which takes a long time to reach perfection – is as expensive as it is: one is paying compound interest for labour and love which is tied up in glass bottles. Many wines, however, mature quickly. A good merchant can suggest a range of wines which are ready for drinking, as well as bigger wines for 'laying down'. While, by buying wines in the year of the harvest can enable one to get them cheaper, one has – apart from having to pay for them – the continual problem of refraining from drinking them too soon. Locking them up and losing the key is, perhaps, the answer.

Generally speaking, Claret takes a long time to mature because of its high tannin content which acts as a preservative. Natural sugar – as in Sauternes and the great German wines – does very much the same, while the 'Pinot Noir', the grape used for the fine wines in Burgundy, produces a slow maturing wine. Most of the lighter, dry white wines are best enjoyed quite young – as freshness is their main quality. Beaujolais – made from the Gamay grape – can be enjoyed the year of the harvest – a 'Beaujolais de l'année', served at cellar temperature, is widely appreciated in France for its flowery freshness. In the last resort, a wine can be drunk as soon as it is nice: experience can guide one, however, as to whether it is likely to get any nicer.

CHAPTER FIVE
French Wines Without Tears

ONE OF THE MOST completely satisfying holidays for the lover of good wines, good food and beautiful countryside is a slow gastronomic tour of the French provinces, which, given careful planning, can be surprisingly inexpensive. It is important to go out of season and to be equipped with the right books to enable one to get the most out of any particular region: AA literature against car sickness, Alexis Lichine's *Wines of France*, Curnonski's *Traditional Recipes of the Provinces of France* and the latest *Guide Michelin* are all to be recommended. It is also important to take plenty of Alka-Seltzer. For the trip to be really successful, one must allow enough time to be able to dawdle and to plan only a rough itinerary – to include whatever regions appeal and a few visits to gastronomic high spots.

Generally, on arriving in an attractive market town or village, one can discover a delightful inn or auberge situated in the nearby countryside by inquiring in any reasonable bar in the middle of the main square. Not long ago, I was driving through the Dordogne with a friend in very early spring: we stopped at an auberge recommended in the *Guide Michelin* to discover it was not yet open, but the owner suggested we find another place three miles further along the river. We were given a room with a balcony overlooking the whole valley and we had a delicious dinner of vegetable soup, omelette aux truffes, confit d'oie aux cêpes and salad, cheese, fruit and coffee. We drank a white wine from Bergerac and the 'black' wine from Cahors. The meal itself cost 18/6 a head. No, I'm *not* going to give the name away.

Certain wine clubs and merchants arrange visits to the big wine producing areas, which is fine if one wants to go about with lots of people. One must watch for a tendency of the Nancy Mitford type francophile to praise all things French with an orgiastic lack of criticism and to behave like de Gaulle about all things British. While the French can – and often do – produce the best food and wine, the most attractive women and the most intelligent writers in the world, it can be pointed out that they also produce the lousiest novels, the most avaricious women, the worst politicians and often keep red wine in the fridge.

CHAPTER SIX
The Vineyards of France

Champagne

OF ALL THE WINES of France, Champagne is the epitome of luxury and gaiety, often suggestive of successful sexual seduction. But before anyone invests in an expensive bottle for this reason, it should be remembered that the champagne manufacturers do not supply any guarantee that their excellent product is an aphrodisiac, even if their salesmen do cherish its reputation. Soft lights and music help, but, in the last resort, the object of one's attractions must feel the same way – in which case Nescafe or a cup of tea can work. Perhaps one could say that champagne helps in bringing matters to a conclusion – one way or the other.

Where Champagne is Made

The capital of the Champagne country is Rheims, a hundred and eighty miles due east of Paris, but most of the vineyards are around Épernay. Almost all Champagne is made by blending the juice of red and white grapes, the Pinot Noir, Pinot Blanc and Chardonnay. Normally, the juice is separated from the pulp as soon as they are pressed, unless a rosé is required in which case the colour from the skins is allowed to seep into the juice itself. Some rather exclusive Cham-

The wine-growing areas of France

pagne is made entirely from the Pinot Blanc, in which case it is called 'Blanc de Blancs'.

How Champagne is Made

After pressing, the wine is allowed to ferment in enormous open vats until mid-winter, when the temperature is lowered to stop the process. The wine is 'racked', cleared of impurities – three times, then, having been cleared, is drawn off and bottled. A dose of sugar, dissolved in wine, is added before the bottle is stoppered with a temporary cork held down by a metal clamp. Then the yeast in the wine acts on the sugar to produce alcohol and carbonic acid gas. As the generated gas cannot escape, the wine becomes bubbly.

This second fermentation takes about four years, whereupon the bottles are put neck downwards in special racks – *pupitres* – and are turned and twisted every day to allow the deposit to collect in the neck of the bottle. The *degorgement* is the highly skilled process of removing the cork and the sediment, tasting the wine, adding some dissolved sugar if the wine is to be sweeter and re-corking. The degrees of sweetness are, from the dryest, *Brut*, *Extra Dry*, *Dry*, *Demi-Sec* and *Doux*. Finally, the wine is labelled, capsuled, packed and despatched – by which time it has been handled by some eighty four highly skilled men. One must ask oneself if a particular girl is worthy of such loving care, and expense, before opening the Dom Perignon.

What Champagne is Produced

There are many firms which produce Champagne. As we have seen, Champagne can be white, rosé, or 'blanc de blancs' and it varies in sweetness. These firms market it in one of two ways. Either the Champagne house is well known enough to be sold under its own name in which case it is known as a 'grande marque'. Or, if it is not well known, the firm sells its Champagne to merchants, who register and sell it under a brand name of their own devising. This Champagne is known in the trade as *BOB* – Buyer's Own Brand – and is cheaper than a grande marque. It can be extremely good if carefully chosen. Finally, most houses – whether grande marque or BOB – not only produce a range of sweetness, a rosé and a blancs de blancs, but also produce vintage and non-vintage wines. The former, obviously, is made from grapes of a particular year, while non-vintage Champagne gives a house the opportunity to produce with skilful blending, an acceptable wine of predictable quality at a low price. A BOB non-vintage Champagne is what is generally considered adequate for debs and their delights. Champagne tends to maderise and become flat with age, and, unless one happens to have a taste for old champagne, it should be drunk during the first ten or twelve years of its life.

Alsace

The vineyards of Alsace lie due south of Strasbourg to the east of Champagne. The wine of the area has had a chequered history, partly because of the eternal wrangle between France and Germany as to who should own the province, and partly because, as in Burgundy, the big estates of the Church were split up among a large number of peasants at the time of the Revolution – who did not have the same respect for quality as did the Benedictine monks. Whenever a wine snob's conversation mentions the wine-producing monasteries, it is useful to remember Saki's bon mot: 'You can say what you like about Christianity: a religion which can produce Green Chartreuse can never really die.'

Anyway, it is only since 1928 that there has been a real attempt to improve quality in Alsatian wines and to market them abroad. Generally, the vignerons sell their produce to a local co-operative, who has a contract with a shipper, merely guaranteeing the grape variety used. A very few shippers produce a single vineyard wine produced from a single grape variety: so far, the market has not been created to buy such wine at a high price. Alsatian wines are always white.

Grape Varieties

SYLVANER:
Light elegant wines, fresh and flowery, which do not keep, make very pleasant inexpensive drinking.
MUSCAT:
Earthy and more highly bouqueted.
PINOT:
Two varieties, the Pinot Blanc and the Pinot Gris (also known as Tokay). The wine has greater body and greater distinction.
RIESLING:
This is a grape of much greater distinction, producing a wine of considerable body and bouquet.
TRAMINER AND GEWURZTRAMINER:
Two varieties of the same grape which sets and ripens earlier than the Riesling. This means that if the harvest is spoilt by bad weather a Traminer will be a better wine than a Riesling, while if the weather is good, a Traminer will over-ripen to produce a naturally sweet, full wine in the manner of Sauternes and the Trockenbeerenauslesen of Germany.

Burgundy

The Burgundy Country lies about a hundred miles due south of the Champagne area, and starts with Chablis, through the Côtes d'Or which includes the great wines of the Côtes de Nuits and the Côtes de

Beaune and ends with Chalonnais, Maconnais and Beaujolais. While Beaujolais cannot be described as Burgundy, it is usually handled by a dealer based in or around Beaune.

The great vineyards of this area were once owned by the Dukes of Burgundy or by the Church and, because of this, the Burgundian wine industry suffered heavily during the Revolution. The vineyards were seized and divided by the *sans culottes* into literally hundreds of small holdings. The peasant proprietors neither had the finance to see them through a bad year, nor perhaps the innate respect for quality: a tradition of evil shortcuts began to become normal – blending, overproducing and false labelling.

In spite of the appellation laws of today, the effects of this tradition are still being felt. When buying a Claret, one can rely on a classified chateau bottled wine being and costing exactly what it should. A Burgundy called *Pommard les Grands Épenots*, for example, may be extremely good and extremely expensive – or not so expensive and not very nice.

One has to have a merchant who deals with the wines of one of the relatively few really good négociants, and be prepared to pay the right price for good wine – there is absolutely no point in paying a medium price for a blended or stretched wine.

Wine drinkers are often divided between those who prefer Burgundy or those who prefer Claret. There is, naturally, no categoric answer to such a subjective argument. Perhaps one could say that the bigness and fullness of Burgundy makes it more easily appreciated by someone who has only recently started drinking wine critically. Ideally, one should be able to have an impartial appreciation of both. Finally, the cuisine of Burgundy is quite superb: *coq au vin*, *boeuf bourguignon* and *escargots de Bourgogne* are world famous specialities.

The Vineyards of Burgundy

Chablis

A true Chablis is quite delicious, greeny-yellow in colour, a hint of blackcurrants in the bouquet and a clean, steely taste which makes it go perfectly with fresh shellfish. The best known vineyards are: Les Vandésirs, Les Clos, Les Grenouilles, Les Preuses, Bougros, Valmur and Les Blanchots. All true Chablis is made from the Pinot grape and the grading is *Chablis Grand-Cru* or *Grands Chablis*, *Chablis Premier Cru* and, simply *Chablis*. The exact vineyards, the yield of the harvest and the alcoholic strength determine which category is which. *Petit Chablis* is a name given to the white vins ordinaires of the district – but they can be quite pleasant.

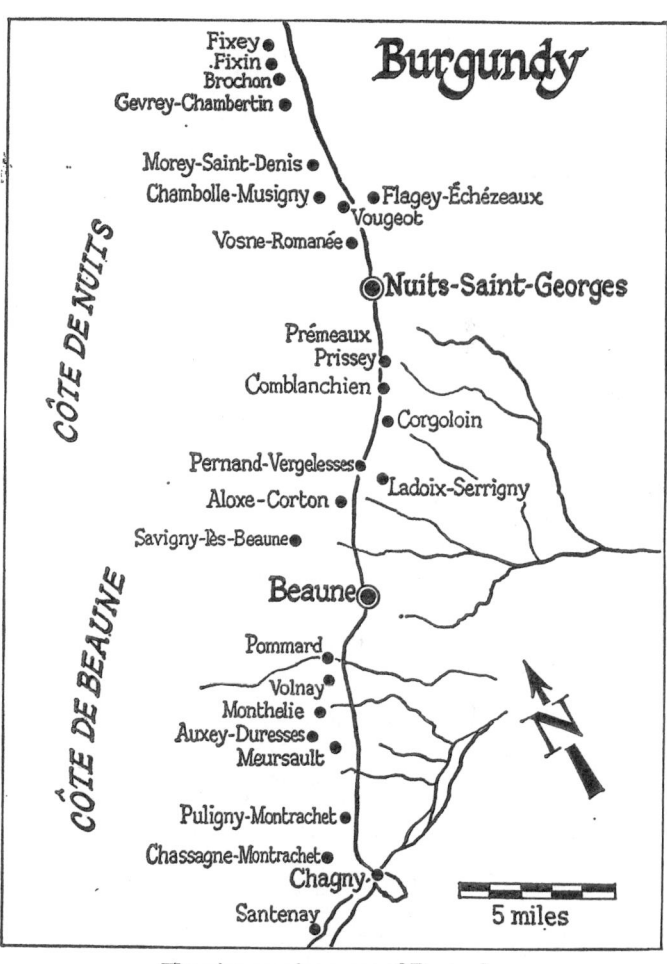

The wine-growing areas of Burgundy

Côte d'or

These wines are produced from the Pinot grape. 'The Golden Coast' refers, presumably, to the price of the wines. This is the name for the area, due south of Chablis, which produces the greatest wines of Burgundy, and it is divided into:
(a) **Côte de Nuits**, which stretches from Fixin to just north of Beaune. The capital is Nuits-Saint-Georges.
(b) **Côte de Beaune**, which goes South as far as Santenay. The capital is Beaune.

Côte de Nuits

Without getting too complicated, the greatest Burgundian red wines come from the Côte de Nuits: full bodied, rich and robust. The villages and main vineyards are:

GEVREY CHAMBERTIN: Le Chambertin and Clos de Bèze
VOUGEOT: Le Clos Vougeot
VOSNE-ROMANÉE: La Romanée Conti, La Romanée St. Vivant, La Romanée, La Tache and Le Richebourg
CHAMBOLLE MUSIGNY: Les Musigny and Les Bonnes Mares
MOREY ST. DENIS: Le Clos de Tart
FLAGEY ÉCHÉZEAUX: Les Grands Échézeaux
NUITS ST. GEORGES: Les St. Georges, Les Pintiers, Les Cailles (et al)
PRÉMEAUX: Le Clos de la Maréchale, Les Corvées (et al)

The names in bold capitals are villages, and a district wine will only bear the name of the village, which can be evocative of a much greater wine than is the case. The *Crus Hors Ligne* are named by the vineyard itself: Le Chambertin, La Romaneé Conti, etc., while the *Premiers Grand Crus* will bear the name of the village, followed by the name of the vineyard: Morey St. Denis, Le Clos de Tart or Nuits St. Georges, Les Pruliers etc. The same system applies to the second and third class vineyards. In other words, the classification in Burgundy is supposed to be from the great *Crus Hors Ligne* to the *Premier Grands Crus*, to the Seconds *Grands Crus* to the *Troisièmes Grands Crus* to the district wines. If you want to know more about all this, buy a bigger book.

Côte de Beaune

The red wines of the Côte de Beaune are softer and more flowery than those of the Côte de Nuits. But the Côte de Beaune produce the greatest white Burgundies. The villages and main vineyards are:

ALOXE CORTON (red): Le Corton, Les Chaumes or Clos du Roi
PERNAUD-VERGELESSES (red): L'Ile de Vergelesses
SAVIGNY-LÈS BEAUNE (red); Les Marconnets

BEAUNE (red): Les Champs Pimonts, Les Grèves
POMMARD (red): Les Épenots, Les Boucherottes
VOLNAY (red): Les Caillerets, La Barre
MEURSAULT (white): Les Perrières, Les Charmes Dessus, Les Genevrières
PULIGNY MONTRACHET (white): Le Montrachet (Hors Lignes): Chevalier and Bâtard Montrachet.
CHASSAGNE MONTRACHET (white): Les Criots.

The classifications are the same as the Côte de Nuits, but a lot of fun can be had in talking to a wine snob about a wine from the Côte de Beaune of the 'wrong' colour: a red Meursault or Chassagne Montrachet or a white Aloxe Corton. You will be quite safe, as they do exist, even if they are difficult to find.

The Côtes Chalonnais, Maconnais and Beaujolais

These vineyards lie along the river Saône due south of the Côte de Beaune, from around Chalon to around Brouilly in the Beaujolais area. The red wines of the Chalonnais and Maconnais are very similar to those of the Côte de Beaune, soft, full and with a beautiful bouquet. The white wines are dry, heady and vigorous. The best growths come from the hamlets of Mercurey, Givry and Montagny for red wine, while the best known white wine comes from Pouilly in the region of Fuissé. Much wine is sold as red or white Macon, just as a lot of rather awful white wine is sold, bogusly, as 'Pouilly Fuissé'.

Beaujolais is treated very badly. Beaujolais is made from the Gamay grape which produces an abundant crop of very fast maturing wine. The wine is fresh, fruity, well bouqueted and of a purple colour, and should be drunk very young at cellar temperature. Because this wine can be produced in quantity and is therefore inexpensive, and because of its charming characteristics and name, Beaujolais has become very popular and demand far exceeds all genuine supply. No wine can be mass-produced and Paris alone consumes more so-called Beaujolais than can be grown in the area itself. This suggests that there must be an awful lot of very odd stuff about masquerading under the name. Some restaurants in France advertise 'Notre nouveau Beaujolais est arrivé' – which means the Beaujolais of the year has arrived. But if the advertisement is signed (in Arabic script) with a name like Abdul Gamal Nasser, it can be suspect: a hell of a lot of Algerian red is imported in tankers to Lyons – heaven knows what this stuff is called by the time it arrives on the table to be drunk.

Some enterprising merchants in England are specialising in importing genuine Beaujolais, and are trying to create a market for the real stuff which will enable them to secure the whole crop of a small producer by paying a proper price for it. It is generally labelled with the name of the villages and the grower: *Julienas, Chenas, Fleurie, Chiroubles, Leynes, St. Amour, Romanéche-Thorins* are among the best known names, while *Moulin à Vent, Morgan* and *Brouilly* are the best known districts. Once more, the consumer has to be able to trust his merchant: all one can say is that the more he commits himself as to what he sells on his labels, the more he is out on a limb. Otherwise, the gradings are *Beaujolais Villages, Beaujolais Superior* and *Beaujolais*. Like everything else, you pays your money and you takes your choice.

The Vineyards of the Rhone and Provence

Very roughly, the further South is a vineyard, the better the weather, the more abundant the crop and the coarser the wine. The wines from the Côtes du Rhone are grown mainly on stony ground, and are deep in colour, distinctive in bouquet, strong in taste, high in alcohol and will last for years. Frequently they are not even bottled for four or five years. The white wines are golden in colour, full bodied and very 'winey', there is one very small vineyard – the Château Grillet – which produces one of the greatest white wines in France. The vignerons from Tavel produce the finest rosé wines: dry, aromatic and full of essential character.

Côte Rôtie: the most northern vineyards of the Rhone, near to Vienne. These vineyards are reputed to date from 600 A.D. and produce the finest red wines in the area.

Condrieu: best known as the area of Château Grillet, where the Loire meets the Rhone.

Hermitage: grown close to the town of Tournon, in very beautiful country, there are adjoining vineyards which produce *Crozes-Hermitage*. The wines are very alcoholic, suitable to be drunk with the strong garlic and tomato tastes of the local food.

Saint Péray: close to Valence, the wines are lighter and are frequently made into sparkling wine in the champagne method.

Châteauneuf du Pape: The best known wines of the area, centred around the ancient city of the Popes, Avignon. Red, white and rosé wines are produced, which are typically heady, warm and powerful. The best wines from the area are sold under the name of individual vineyards: *Chateaux Fortia, de la Nerthe, Vaudrieu,* etc.

Tavel: these fine rosés come from around Roquemaure close to Avignon. The red and white wines are blended in with other local areas but the rosés, because of their quality, have their own appellation.

Lesser Known Wines of France

There are a very few enterprising merchants in Britain who specialise in discovering and importing French wines from districts which are not well known. If these wines are carefully chosen, they can be quite delightful in and of themselves, apart from being of geographic interest. Among such wines are:

Wines of Arbois

These wines come from the Jura district and include pleasant red, white and rosés for everyday use. Better known is *Vin Jaune* which is matured for at least six years before being sold, and the *Vin de Paille* which is fermented like sherry, of high alcoholic strength and will improve over the years.

Wines of Gaillac

These wines are grown in the country of Toulouse-Lautrec, near Albi, and have pleasant flinty characteristics. Around this area is produced plenty of rather ordinary sparkling wine, which can be mixed with other things for parties and summer drinking.

Wines of the Dordogne

One of the most delightful areas in France to enjoy some of the best cooking, the wines are pleasant, without being special. *Montbazillac* is a naturally sweet, but coarser, version of Sauternes while *Bergerac* is dryer and cleaner. The 'black' wine of Cahors, further east, is pungent, aromatic and woody in flavour. These sorts of wine are sufficiently interesting to be worth bullying your merchant into obtaining. He should know where they can be found in London.

The Brandies of France

'An auction of brandy was proceeding without incident, when a man at the front of the hall suddenly took out his handkerchief and began to wipe his forehead. Then he sighed, clapped his hand to his chest, and sat down. There was a sympathetic murmur. "Taken ill . . . poor chap . . . looks pretty dicky . . ." Feebly, the sick man cried, "Brandy! Brandy!" A gentleman in the front row who had just seen twelve dozen knocked down to him could hardly refuse aid. With grudging chivalry, he uncorked a bottle and handed it to the patient. "I think . . . a little air," said the patient, and, getting to his feet, he walked to the back of the hall. "Is there a doctor here?" shouted the auctioneer. It didn't much matter whether there was or not. The patient had got a flying start. Once near the exit door, the sick man seemed to revive, and before anybody could ask if

he was feeling better, he had slipped out, and was off down the street like a wing three quarter with the wind behind him. What he hugged was no ball, but a bottle. And the word "Foulenough" was already being whispered in the hall which he had left so unceremoniously.'

(The Best of Beachcomber)

This is a very inexpensive way of acquiring brandy. Christies have regular auctions, details of which can be obtained by writing in.

How Brandy is Made

Brandy is the general name given to the spirit which is distilled from grapes, and is produced all over the world wherever grapes are grown. And very nasty a lot of it is, too. The French spirit production is divided between Cognac, Armagnac and Marc – all of which are made from grapes, and the 'eaux de vie' which are distillations from other fruit.

Cognac

Cognac is produced, appropriately enough, around the town of Cognac due north of Bordeaux. It is made mainly from the Folle Blanche Grape. The best Cognac is produced closest to the town and is allowed to call itself *Grande Champagne*, while the next best area around it is called *Petite Champagne*. The word champagne has no connection whatsoever with the wine. '*Fine Champagne*' is a mixture of the two. The other Cognac districts produce brandy of a lower calibre.

The distillation is carried out in a 'Charente' still and Cognac is aged in casks of Limousin oak, which, traditionally, give it its colour. Brandy must be given time to mature, which is done by allowing it to stay in cask for many years, gradually losing its fieriness and becoming mellow and aromatic.

Theoretically, Three Star brandy is five years old. V.S.O. (Very Superior Old) is brandy from twelve to seventeen years old. V.S.O.P. (Very Superior Old Pale) is brandy from eighteen to twenty-five years old, V.V.S.O.P. (Very Very Superior Old Pale) is brandy from twenty five to forty years old.

In fact, of course, demand has far exceeded supply, and the big houses in Cognac blend their brandies of various age, add vanilla and colouring matter and use the symbols merely as a commercial guide. The habit of blending is so widespread now, that French wine laws forbid a manufacturer to sell a cognac with a particular year on the bottle. One can occasionally find some genuine vintage brandy at auctions or in the cellars of some small growers in the area. The only trouble is that it is grotesquely expensive. Perhaps the best buy is the pale, fine Cognac of good origin which is more expensive than Three Star, but cheaper than V.S.O.P. Such cognac is clean, pale and unflavoured with vanilla. Being young, it can be fiery, but so what? Anyway, I prefer Scotch.

Armagnac

Armagnac is produced in the extreme south of Gascony, using a slightly different system of manufacture and cask, but the same grape, as Cognac. The trade is far less established – D'Artagnan's descendant, the Marquis de Montesquieu has done much to improve things – and this can enable a clever merchant to pick up an excellent Armagnac at proportionately a lower price than a Cognac. By the same token, of course, he can come the most awful cropper.

Marc

Marc is the general name given to brandy produced in the other wine areas of France. Thus you get a Marc de Borgogne, a Marc de Champagne, a Marc de la Loire, etc. If it is carefully made and well aged, Marc can have an earthy charm of its own. It is always acceptable if you have a nostalgic need to remember the flavour of that charming little town in Provence where you were so happy with some one who has subsequently left you, or if, of course, you happen to like paying quite a lot for a drink that tastes like a mixture of old boots and turpentine.

Eaux de Vie

The Eaux de Vies are much more fun. They are the general name given all over France to spirits made from other fruit, but by more or less the same process as brandy. Again, some merchants are rooting out good producers of reasonable aged booze. The price is about the same as commercial V.S.O.P. cognac, and can be much more interesting after dinner.

CALVADOS: produced in Normandy, out of apples, is known by Americans as 'Apple Jack Brandy'. It should be well aged, and can be delicious if used in cooking certain Norman dishes.

REINE CLAUDE: A white eaux de vie made from greengages.

POIRE WILLIAM: A white eaux de vie made from pears (particularly good).

MIRABELLE: A white eaux de vie made from plums.

FRAMBOISE: A white eaux de vie made from raspberries.

And so on. You name a fruit and in all probability the French make it into brandy. The white eaux de vie should be served well chilled.

The wine-growing areas of Bordeaux

The Vineyards of Bordeaux

Claret

Claret is the English name for the red wines which come from around Bordeaux, on the South western coast of France. As capital of the province of Gascony, Bordeaux was an English possession for some three hundred years – which established a traditional acceptance of its wines. Claret is known as the 'Englishman's wine', and our wine trade has deeply rooted affiliations with Bordeaux, enabling us to import properly made and classified wines of guaranteed quality far more easily than, say, from Burgundy. Anglo-Saxon, or perhaps Celtic names can be found among the most distinguished chateaux: Smith, Palmer, Brown, Barton, Lynch, Montrose, Boyd, and Talbot amongst them.

The Character of the Wines

Claret is a very different wine from Burgundy. The full bodied bigness of Burgundy makes it far easier to appreciate for the beginner than the dry sophistication of Claret. A multitude of sins can be covered by additives – sugar, spirit, sulphur or lime – which are not allowed into good Claret. Pure grape juice with a high tannin content produces the characteristic of longevity. Young claret is quite disgustingly 'green', and wines of extraordinary age can still be enjoyed. The late Maurice Healey claims to have enjoyed a Lafite 1811 in 1926 – 115 years old, but the inexorable pressure of finance will, I suppose, eventually price naturally aged claret out of the market.

Another reason for the popularity of claret among wine lovers is the variety of qualities produced by the varied proportions of a variety of grapes used in one area: whereas red Burgundy comes from the Pinot Noir, claret is produced from the Cabernet, Malbec, Merlot and Verdot grapes. A really good claret has an intellectual astringency of quality in bouquet, finesse and vinosity. As, say, oysters or Stilton cheese are essences of food taste, so is claret an essence in wine – scorning to use 'sauces' or 'aromatics' to cover deficiencies.

The Areas and Classifications in Bordeaux

The wines of Bordeaux are grown around the river Gironde and its tributaries: Garonne and Dordogne. Starting north-west of Bordeaux and proceeding anti-clockwise, the main areas are:

The Médoc

The home of the finest clarets, this area is divided into the Haut Médoc and the Bas Médoc. The five principle producers of the Médoc can be defined in quality:

Finesse	Body	Vinosity
1. Margaux	1. Pauillac	1. St. Estèphe
2. Cantenac	2. St. Julien	2. Pauillac
3. Pauillac	3. St. Estèphe	3. St. Julien
4. St. Julien	4. Cantenac	4. Cantenac
5. St. Estèphe	5. Margaux	5. Margaux

To guide and control the prices of Médoc wines, there was an official classification in 1855, for the Paris Universal Exhibition of that year.

PREMIER GRANDS CRUS

Château Lafite	Rothschild, Pauillac
Château Latour	Pauillac
Château Margaux	Margaux

SECONDS GRANDS CRUS

Château Mouton Rothschild, Pauillac	Most people consider this wine deserves to be upgraded to first growth
Château Rausan-Ségla	Margaux
Château Rauzan-Gassies	Margaux
Château Léoville-Lascases	St. Julien
Château Léoville Poyferre	St. Julien
Château Léoville-Barton	St. Julien
Château Durfort-Vivens	Margaux
Château Lascombes	Margaux
Château Gruaud-Larose	St. Julien
Château Brane-Cantenac	Cantenac
Château Pichon-Longueville	Pauillac
Château Pichon-Longueville – Comtesse de La Lande	Pauillac
Château Ducru-Beaucaillou	St. Julien
Château Cos d'Estournel	St. Estèphe
Château Montrose	St. Estèphe

TROISIEMES GRANDS CRUS

Château Kirwan	Cantenac
Château d'Issan	Cantenac
Château Lagrange	St. Julien
Château Langoa	St. Julien
Château Giscours	Labarde

Château Malescot St.-Exupéry	Margaux
Château Cantenac Brown	Cantenac
Château Palmer	Cantenac
Châtaeu La Lagune	Ludon
Château Desmirail	Margaux
Château Calon Ségur	St.-Estèphe
Château Ferrière	Margaux
Château Marquis d'Alesme-Becker	Margaux
Château Boyd Cantenac	Margaux

QUATRIEMES GRANDS CRUS

Château St.-Pierre Bontemps	St.-Julien
Château St.-Pierre Sevaistre	St.-Julien
Château Branaire Ducru	St.-Julien
Château Talbot	St.-Julien
Château Duhart Milon	Pauillac
Château Pouget	Cantenac
Château La Tour Carnet	St.-Laurent
Château Rochet	St.-Estèphe
Château Beychevelle	St.-Julien
Château Le Prieuré	Cantenac
Château Marquis de Terme	Margaux

CINQUIEMES GRANDS CRUS

Château Pontet-Canet	Pauillac
Château Batailley	Pauillac
Château Haut-Batailley	Pauillac
Château Grand Puy Lacoste	Pauillac
Château Grand Puy Ducasse	Pauillac
Château Lynch Bages	Pauillac
Château Lynch Moussas	Pauillac
Château Dauzac	Labarde
Château Mouton d'Armailhacq (or Château Baron Philippe)	Pauillac
Château Le Tertre	Arsac
Château Haut Bages Liberal	Pauillac
Château Pedesclaux	Pauillac
Château Belgrave	St.-Laurent
Château Camensac	St.-Laurent
Château Cos Labory	St.-Estéphe
Château Cler Milon	Pauillac
Château Croizet Bages	Pauillac
Château Cantemerle	Macau

Due South of the Médoc, lies the Graves – an area best known for the dry white wines. The red wines, however, are excellent and Château Haut Brion is rated as good as first growths from the Médoc.

Classified Growths of Red Wines from the Graves

Château Haut-Brion, Léognan This wine is regarded as one of the great first growths.

Château Haut Billy	Léognan
Château La Mission Haut-Brion	Pessac
Château Latour Haut-Brion	Talence
Château Carbonnieux	Léognan
Domaine de Chevalier	Léognan
Château Malartic-Lagravière	Léognan
Château Olivier	Léognan
Château Latour-artillac	Martillac
Château Smith-Haut-Lafitte	Martillac
Château Bouscaut	Cadaujac
Château Pape Clément	Pessac
Château Fieuzal	Léognan

Classified Growths of White Wines from the Graves

Château Carbonnieux	Léognan
Château Bouscaut	Cadaujac
Château Chevalier	Léognan
Château Olivier	Léognan
Château Laville Haut-Brion	Pessac and Talence
Château Malartic-Lagravière	Léognan
Château Couhins	Villenave-d'Ornon
Château La Tour-Marcillac	Martillac

Sauternes

South of Graves is the home of that great sweet white wine which some females seem to enjoy drinking with almost any food. The habit of drinking sweet white wine with puddings is dying in a calorie-conscious society, and sauternes can be disgustingly sickly when compared to some of the German wines. However, the technique of making a naturally sweet wine is of interest. The Sauvignon grape is only picked when it is over-ripe to a point of rottenness – the pourriture noble, but the timing has to be perfect, if the crop is not to be lost. This means the harvest has to be covered and re-covered if the grapes are to be picked 'au moment critique' – an expensive process.

Classification of Sauternes

PREMIERS GRANDS CRUS
Château D'Yquem Regarded as a great first growth.

PREMIER CRUS

Château La Tour Blanche	Bommes
Château Lafaurie-Peyraguey	Bommes
Clos Haut-Peyraguey	Bommes
Château Rayne-Vigneau	Bommes
Château Rabaud-Promis	Bommes
Château Suduiraut	Preignac
Château Coutet	Barsac
Château Climens	Barsac
Château Guiraud	Sauternes
Château Rieussec	Fargues
Château Rabaud-Sigalas	Bommes

DEUXIEMES CRUS

Château Doisy Daene	Barsac
Château Dubroca	Barsac
Château Doisy Védrines	Barsac
Château Filhot	Sauternes
Château Myrat	Barsac
Château d'Arche	Sauternes
Château Broustet	Barsac
Château Caillou	Barsac
Château Suau	Barsac
Château de Malle	Preignac
Château Romer Lafon	Fargues
Château Romer de la Miremory	Fargues
Château Lamothe	Sauternes
Château d'Arch Lafaurie	Sauternes
Château Nairac	Barsac

Entre Deux Mers

This district lies east of Sauternes, between the Garonne and Dordogne rivers. Red and white wines are produced here, but, nothing of any importance. The wines are usually used for vins ordinaires.

St. Emilion

Very good red wines come from this area north of the Dordogne River. They have plenty of body and fullness, which make them a little like a Burgundy, and are considered generally comparable in quality to a fifth growth Médoc.

Classification of St. Émilion
PREMIERS GRANDS CRUS CLASSES
Château Ausone
Château Cheval Blanc
Château Beauséjour (Dufau)   Château La Gaffelière-Naudes
Château Beauséjour (Fagouet) Château Magdelaine
Château Belair   Château Pavie
Château Canon   Château Trottevieille
Château Figeac   Clos Fourtet

North of the Dordogne River, from Fronsac to Cubzac, Bourg, and Blaye, a great deal of ordinary red and white wine is produced of indifferent quality and which is used for *vins ordinaires* or blending.

Bourgeois Growths

These clarets are the wines of châteaux not officially classified. Their price, therefore, is much lower and, if well made and bottled, can be very good buys. Once again, ask your wine merchant. The established London shippers of claret generally have an excellent selection of such wines which they bottle themselves.

The Loire

This is the last important wine producing area of France in our clockwise journey from Paris. North of the Loire, in Normandy, only cider and calvados are produced. One of the most beautiful rivers in France, the Loire runs some three hundred miles from the northern Rhone in a vast curve through the centre, coming to the sea at Nantes, just South of Brittany. The best wines from the Loire are white: the Rosé d'Anjou is merely a pleasant summer drink and the reds are either very ordinary, or, in the case of Borgeuil and Chinon, rather like a bourgeois growth Claret.

Nivernais

Two famous and delicious white wines come from a small area between Cosne and Nevers. On the right bank of the Loire is produced the famous Pouilly Blanc Fumé – not to be confused with Pouilly Fuissé. This wine is made from the Sauvignon grape, and the vineyards are around Pouilly-sur-Loire. The wine is big, clean, dry and delicious. From the other side of the river comes another famous wine, also from the Sauvignon grape: Sancerre.

Touraine

The area, as its name implies, around Tours: many excellent white wines are produced from the Chenin Blanc grape, most famous of which is Vouvray. This wine can vary in sweetness, and some are naturally sparkling. The particular characteristic of Vouvray is slow maturing and long keeping. There is also a definite flavour of quinces.

Anjou

The 'Rosé d'Anjou de Cabernet' is enormously popular: pretty light scented and slightly sweet, it is a very nice poovish wine. Much of it is imported into England, so there must be a market. There are also some heady and alcoholic white wines grown around Saumur, which are not so well known.

Nantes and Brittany

A delicious dry, pale, fresh white wine is grown from the Muscadet grape in the vineyards around Nantes. Muscadet has a freshness of the sea – almost a saltiness – which makes it very suitable to be drunk with oysters and shellfish. Even a French bottled Muscadet is not expensive and is of very good value.

CHAPTER SEVEN
German Wine

THE WINE TRADE has, in its time, dreamt up many more effective sales boosts than having two world wars in fifty years. Before 1914, German wines were, proportionately to overall wine consumption, much more popular than they are today. But a dislike of Kaiser Bill and Hitler are not the only reasons: Edward VII made German spas in the Black Forest fashionable and our own Royal Family kept a closer link with their German cousins. This closer connection with Germany meant that trips down the Rhine were a fashionable type of holiday, which in its turn gave German names and words a familiarity they no longer have.

One of the enormous stumbling blocks to understanding and enjoying German wines is the unpronounceable unfamiliarity of almost all words on the label. One tends to feel frightened of asking for an unfamiliar wine and of getting it wrong, which is a pity because Germany produces some of the greatest white wine in the world. Nor is it necessary to be nervous of a wine snob trumpeting about *Trockenbeerenauslesen*. One can safely admit to not drinking much German wine, not because of cost – with a saintly, forgiving smile – but because one's grandmother was a Cohen.

The History of German Wines

The Romans planted vineyards in Germany nearly two thousand years ago, before, indeed, they were keen to grow wine elsewhere in their Empire. Whereas Italy always produced wine in abundance, there was a shortage of grain, but no one considered the hills either side of the Rhine to be suitable for anything except viticulture. In the course of time, as everywhere else, the best vineyards belonged to kings, princes, barons and the Church. The enthusiasm, incidentally, of the Church for wine was not entirely in wanting to live lives as merry monks: there was an ever present need for sacramental wine, which should to some extent justify the sacraments even to atheists.

Early in the middle ages, England established friendly trading relations with Germany and gave her merchants favourable facilities for business. 'Rhenish' wine, often exported from Hochheim in the heart of the Rheingau – hence the name *hock*, became very popular and established its reputation as a top quality wine with remarkable ageing qualities.

It was Napoleon who caused the first major upheaval in the German wine trade. At the treaty of Lunéville in 1803, he secularised the religious orders, dispossessed some large landowners and distributed the vineyards among small growers. One can see a fascinating contrast between the character of the German small farmer and his French counterpart, who had had the same process of redistribution during the Revolution.

The French tended to allow their passion for profit and inability to work together to lead them to lower their quality by overproduction and short cuts, while the Germans, with their meticulous and painstaking talent for organisation, started passing laws to control wine production. From 1830, the Germans became 'appellation' and classification conscious, while the French started controls only in the 20th Century. The German wine laws are rigidly enforced, which means, from one point of view, that if we can come to terms with the awful words on the labels, the whole set up is far easier to grasp than with French wine. One is saying, in other words, that the German characteristic of being easily regimented, which is *such* a bore in wartime, is rather good when it comes to wine.

The Quality and Types of German Wine

White Wine

The really good wine from Germany is white and comes in the familiar long thin bottles. As will be seen, the meticulous details on the labels can give a very complete history of whatever wine is in the bottle. One can learn:

(a) The village of the district

(b) The vineyard.
(c) The owner's name.
(d) The type of harvesting.
(e) The owner's seal of approval.
(f) The number of the cask which matured the wine.
(g) Where the wine was bottled.
(h) The year of the harvest and
(i) The grape variety.

If a label has all this sort of guff on it, you can be sure that it is a very special wine, made with very special care which sells at a very special price. Great emphasis is put on how the wine is harvested, and the greatest wines are made, like Sauternes, from over-ripe grapes producing a naturally sweet wine, which needs to be drunk by itself, without food. There is no tradition of producing what we would call a 'dry' wine like Chablis or Muscadet. A knowledge of German would help one to recognise when a wine carries a brand or generic name. Liebfraumilch and Niersteiner Domtal are two well known examples of such blends. Like Beaujolais, the quality of such wines will depend, entirely, on the shipper. Similarly, a knowledge of the different districts and their wines is the only way of really establishing a knowledge of what is what.

Red Wine and Rosé

A little rosé and a surprising amount of red wine – from the Burgundy grape – is produced and consumed in Germany itself. The quality, however, is not – price for price – comparable with French wine.

German 'Champagne' or Sekt

A sparkling white wine is made extensively in Germany by a process similar to Champagne, but, instead of being done in individual bottles, it is done in huge vats. This, obviously, cuts the price down considerably. Not surprisingly, the wine is not nearly so nice, either. Sekt is OK for parties or as a basis of a cocktail, but not much else.

German Brandy

Brandy is made by a process similar to that of Cognac, but is nastier. Cheap to drink in Germany itself, the duties of export make it pointless to consider.

The Classification of German Wine

As we have seen, German wine laws rigidly control what appears on a label. The first name is the village, then the vineyard, then the grape

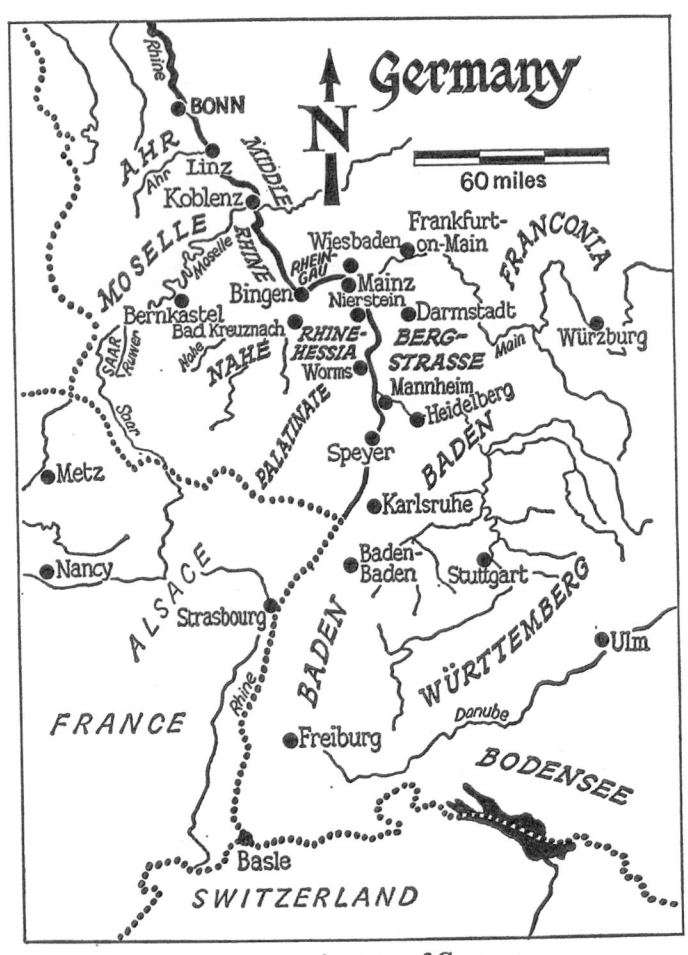

The wine-growing areas of Germany

variety, then the method of harvesting which may be, in ascending order of sweetness:

SPATLESE
Late gathered harvest, with considerable natural sweetness.

AUSLESE
Selected overripe bunches of grapes from a late harvest.

BEERENAUSLESE and TROCKENBEERENAUSLESE:
Selected overripe individual grapes, in the case of Trockenbecvenauslese dried by the sun into raisins, almost.

The labour involved in such selection, and the small yield of juice from overripe berries makes, obviously, these wines very expensive.

EISWEIN (ICE WINE)
When a late, dry summer is followed by a quick, hard frost, the juice in the grapes may become frozen. If the grapes are gathered and pressed while the juice is still frozen, the resultant wine is, most extraordinarily, absolutely superb. The climatic conditions, however, don't often happen: There have been only ten vintages of Eiswein in the last hundred years.

KABINETT
This word has no official legal authority. It merely means that the grower considers this wine to be especially good. This does not, however, mean that the wine has been estate bottled. The vigneron may put the 'Fass' or 'Fuder' number on the label, which refers to different casks of quality. In any one year, he may make three or four different wines of varying quality and sweetness, rather than the general brew up so common in France.

EXAMPLES OF ALL THIS
Deidesheimer Leinhöhle Riesling Trockenbeerenauslese (von Bruhl) 1953 = a wine made in 1953 from selected overripe individual berries of the Reisling vine, grown by a chap called von Bruhl who has a bit of a vineyard called Leinhöle by the town of Deidesheim in the Palatinate.

Kreuznacher Hinkelstein Riesling Spötlese 1959 (estate bottling Anheuser) = a wine made and estate bottled in 1959 from a late gathered harvest of Riesling Grapes by Herr Anheuser, who owns some of the Hinkelstein vineyard by the village of Bad Kreuznach in the Nahe area.

And so on and so forth....

German Grapes and the Harvest

The Germans, with customary thoroughness, are much more scientific than anyone else in the production of wine. As they suffer from a dodgier climate than other wine-producing countries, they are always trying to produce a wine which can withstand unreliable weather. The greatest grape is the Riesling, the strongest and most prolific is the Sylvaner, and they are always experimenting with grafts of the two. Also to be found are the Traminer and Gewurztraminer, the Pinot noir and blanc, and Muscat grapes, amongst others.

While science can help enormously in securing and improving the production of wine, even German scientists have failed to control the climate: most German wine is a pleasant, and light *vin ordinaire*, suitable for quenching thirst. The fuss made over a special wine of a special year is because it is rare. The Germans themselves say that a great wine is as rare as a great statesman – and *what* could be rarer than that?

The Vineyards of Germany

The German vineyards lie alongside the Rhine and her tributaries: Moselle, Ahr, Nahe, Lahn, Main, Neckar and Saar. From this one can realise that a working knowledge of German geography would help one to understand it better. The main areas in descending quality of production are as follows:

(i) **Moselle – Saar – Ruwer** } These are, equally, the best.
(ii) **Rheingau**
(iii) **Rheinhessen** – more wine, less quality.
(iv) **Palatinate (Rheinpfalz)** – still more wine of lesser quality than above.
(v) **Nahe** – good wine, but not as good as that of the Rheingau.
(vi) **Franconia** – a lot of pleasant, everyday wine of little distinction, and a little very good wine indeed.
(vii) **The Mittelrhein** and **Württemberg – Baden Baden** areas produce masses of ordinary wine of little distinction. Cheap to buy, it is possible, however, to discover some charming wines for everyday drinking.

Having said this much, if anyone wants to know more about German wine let them read *The Great Wines of Germany* by Andre Simon and S. F. Hallgarten. Mr. Wolfe is not paying me enough to justify copying out forty-eight pages of explosive sounding German place names: The whole thing is far too reminiscent of having to do lines at school.

CHAPTER EIGHT
Wines of Spain
Sherry

WHILE THERE ARE SO many sorts of sherry that they can be drunk throughout a meal, normally they are drunk as aperitifs. Sherry is the fortified wine from Jerez... Jerez (hence 'Sherry') de la Frontera, in Southern Spain. Fortification is a process of adding brandy to the maturing wine which halts the process of fermentation from sugar into alcohol and gives the resultant wine its qualities of strength and longevity. Fortification will leave natural sugar unconverted to produce a sweet wine, while if the wine is to be dry, fermentation must be vigorous enough to convert all the sugar into alcohol before fortification.

It is a peculiarity of sherry that dryness is achieved by manufacture rather than harvesting methods. There are two distinct types of Sherry produced from any one harvest. The best is called *Fino* which is pale, delicate and light, while the other *Raya* is darker, fuller and coarser. The difference is caused by the unpredictable action of bacteria, called 'Flor' which grows on the surface of some casks and which acts on the wine very much like the white of egg acts on a broth – clarifying and bringing a brilliance to the final soup. The types of Sherry can best be described by a diagram.

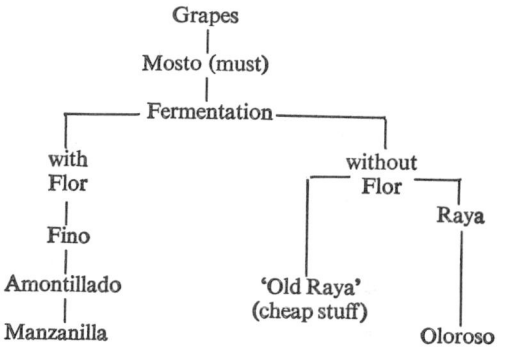

The Solera System

There is no such thing as 'vintage' sherry. For many years the shippers of Sherry have built up a system in their cellars or *Bodegas* of allowing different vintages of different types of Sherry to mature in vats or *Soleras* independently. When they receive an order for so many cases of sherry, they blend different types and vintages of wine to produce an absolutely constant quality. This process of 'averaging out' involves enormous experience and a lot of handling to ensure a regular production of adequately aged wine – which must be the hallmark of good sherry.

The Types of Sherry

FINO
These wines are pale, delicate and delicious, of the highest quality.
MANZANILLA
A Fino which has been matured close to the sea, is dryer – even salty. Both these wines are best served chilled.
AMONTILLADO
A medium sweet nutty wine, whose characteristics result from a well aged 'fat' Fino. This is a compromise between a true Fino and an Oloroso.
OLOROSO
A full, sweet, dark and nutty wine from a matured Raya. Sherry is produced by shippers, some of whom like Gonzalez, Byass, or Pedro Domecq are sold under their own label. Others sell to the British wine trade who sell the Sherry under their own labels. True Sherry comes from Jerez in Spain: 'Cyprus' or 'South African' Sherry is merely a fortified wine made in a similar way by people who need to plagiarise the name because they can't produce a fine enough wine to justify itself with its own name. The reason they can get away with it is because Spain herself only defined the Sherry production area in 1932, and, since then, there has been no satisfactory trading agreement between Spain and Britain.

Table Wines of Spain

Spain, however, steals other people's names: 'Spanish' champagne, 'Spanish' chablis, 'Spanish' Burgundy etc. These wines are marketed in England as being rather characteristic of the French originals. In fact, the resemblance is tenuous in the extreme and they can merely be judged, in relation to price, as ordinary table wines.

The Spirits and Liqueurs of Spain

Spain produces, under licence, a range of liqueurs made to French recipe. These are never exported, but one can, if one wants to go blind, get genuine absinthe – which might be an attraction to admirers of Oscar Wilde. Spanish brandy – Fundador – is very cheap, very strong and very nasty. Because of duty, it is seldom imported into Britain, but much of the abuse of General Franco on the Costa del Sol is not caused by political idealism but merely because of Fundador. One of the nastiest experiences I've ever had was getting drunk on a mixture of Spanish absinthe and Fundador – equal quantities, on the rocks. This subtle and delicious drink is called 'Son-y-Sondra', and should be avoided.

CHAPTER NINE
Wines of Portugal
Port
AS SHERRY IS to Spain, so is port to Portugal, our oldest ally. Port has been shipped from Oporto in quantity since the early eighteenth century, and the name has been well protected: Similar wines from other countries have to be described as 'port style.' Always popular with the English, Port is grown in the upper reaches of the River Douro, in the Minho area in North Portugal. The fortification of Port is done by adding Portuguese brandy to the wine – while it is still fermenting. This preserves its sweetness, and stops the chemical process of fermentation being completed, which produces a tendency for vintage Port to throw a deposit. Most Port is red, and is made from red grapes; white Port is produced from white grapes and can vary in sweetness.

Types of Port
VINTAGE PORT
As its name implies, the product of a great year. Dark red in colour, the wine is bottled in its second year in cask. Still developing, it matures very slowly in bottle, gradually ridding itself of impurities by throwing the characteristic deposit which necessitates such careful handling and decanting before serving. A 'pipe' – about 750 bottles – of young vintage port was a very popular christening present for a boy, as twenty-one years is the ideal length of time for maturing.

CRUSTED OR VINTAGE CHARACTER PORT
This is a blend of several different years but treated as 'vintage' port. 'Vintage Character' port is held for six or more years in cask, which allows the wine to mature much more quickly than in bottle. Impurities are strained off, leaving a wine lighter, but similar to the 'vintage'. Only the best ports are treated in this way – to overcome the problems of ageing true vintage port, but to get a similar product.

TAWNY PORT
This wine is blended and matured in cask, like 'vintage character' – but not for so long. Very pleasant, is more suitable for dodgy livers.

RUBY PORT

This is a blend of early bottled, inferior wines – generally served in public houses, mixed with lemon. When good, it can mature into 'tawny.'

WHITE PORT

Made from white grapes, white port varies in sweetness and should be served chilled as an aperitif.

The practice of fortifying – or stopping the fermentation of the wine by adding brandy – has, in fact, reduced the popularity of port. Arrested fermentation produces a heavy, impure and alcoholic wine, which makes the drinker both fat and ill. We are more sensitive about such things than we were in the eighteenth century.

Portuguese Table Wines

Very sensibly, the government is trying to market Portuguese table wines as wines in their own right, not as Portuguese 'Liebfraumilch' or 'Tavel'. Cheap and good everyday table wines come from Dao, Evel and Colares, while naturally 'petillant' roses and dry white wines called 'vinho verde' are becoming increasingly popular. Sneered at by some – perhaps because of the fancy labels and bottles – the most valid criticism is that they tend to be rather expensive for what they are – a result of having to ship them in bottle.

Other Fortified Wines

MADEIRA

The Portuguese-owned Atlantic island of Madeira produces the fortified wine once known as 'Malmsey' wine. It was in a bath of this wine that a Duke of Clarence in the Middle Ages was drowned – what a lovely way to go. No. Cancel that. Quite horrible. Madeira is artificially heated after its first fermentation, and before the addition of cane brandy, which gives it its special bitter-sweet taste. The wines are classified by grape varieties, in ascending order of sweetness *Sercial*, *Verdelho*, *Boal* and *Malmsey*. The lighter, dryer wines may be drunk at any time, while a heavy and sweet Malmsey should be served after food. The special characteristic of Madeira is its long life: one can still occasionally find and enjoy a wine produced in the eighteenth century.

MALAGA

A dark, heavy, fortified wine is produced in the Spanish town of that name – but it was more popular in Victorian times than today.

MARSALA

Nelson's fleet acquired a taste for this sticky stuff from Marsala in Sicily. I find it pointless except for the cooking of Zabaione or escalopini a la Marsala. Perhaps the Mafia enjoy it.

CHAPTER TEN
The Wines of Italy

BEING MUCH MORE interested in singing, eating pasta and making love, the Italians – very sensibly – have merely demanded enormous quantities of wine to swig, without wasting time with one-upmanship. Indeed, an Italian chef I know treads his own wine. As the grapes come from Covent Garden, and his house is in Shepherd's Bush, I presume he is going to sell it as *Chianti di Goldhawk Road*, in bottles covered with straw filched from the BBC.

Anyway, the main point about Italian wine is to remember that there is an enormous amount of it, and it is meant to be swigged with cheerful familiarity, and rumbustious food. Most of it is produced in Northern Italy. The baking sun of the South affects the grapes, and the resultant wine is generally used for blending.

We can, however, expect an improvement in future: the latest Italian wine laws, passed in 1963, have started the process of definition and classification so necessary for the production of quality wines. As the Italians have so successfully exported their food all over the world, it is rather surprising that they have not had these laws before. Perhaps they have relied on the attraction of straw-covered bottles to sell wine.

Very briefly, Piedmont produces *Asti Spumante*, which is a rather nasty sweet sparkling wine only suitable for wine cups or Buck Fizz. It also produces *Barolo*, which is quite one of the best red wines of Italy. Around the city of Turin is the production of *Vermouth, Martini, Cinzano, Carpano, Campari, Gancia* and others. Perhaps the nicest is the rather bitter *Punt E Mes*.

From the Veneto comes a pleasant red wine – *Valpolicella*, which is made around Lake Garda and a good dry white wine – *Soave* – from around Verona.

Chianti comes from Tuscany and is made by the 'Governo' system to produce a second fermentation. This enhances the quality of a wine meant to be drunk young. It is almost the only area where much of the wine is grown on large, private estates: their modern methods of viticulture have produced a consistently reasonable quality and enormous quantity. That, with the wicker bottles, has made Chianti seem synonomous for Italian wine.

These are only a very few of the best known Italian wines. There are masses of others, and lots of improbable legends about them. If anyone is particularly interested, Cyril Ray has written an excellent book called, appropriately, *The Wines of Italy*.

CHAPTER ELEVEN
The Wines of the Rest of the World

APART FROM the fortified wines of the Iberian Peninsular – sherry and port – the wines from other countries do not compare in importance with the great wines of France and Germany. They do produce, however, very pleasant everyday table wines as good, if not better, than some French and German vins ordinaires. There are two main reasons for this:

Climate

Apart from a few relatively obscure European wines (Russsian, Hungarian, Rumanian) most other wine producing countries enjoy a lot of sunshine, which ensures an abundant crop of fairly coarse wine. The great wines of France and Germany come from the northern-most limits of the wine growing areas, which appears to give the vigneron subtle qualities in his wine to compensate for lack of crop.

Marketing Methods and Problems

A general recognition of the great qualities of French and German wines has led, over the ages, to an established classification and system of world wide marketing which enables the vigneron to benefit, financially, by taking enormous care in his methods of manufacture. Such wines have always been able to command top prices. The growers in the rest of Europe, generally peasant farmers, have been able to produce wine only for local consumption where cheap quantity rather than expensive quality has been the demand.

Out of Europe, the best wines from younger vineyards have been reserved almost exclusively for extremely private consumption. If anyone has to visit the wine growing areas of South Africa, Australia or the Americas, it is well worth insisting on sampling the best local produce: transport costs alone prohibit the sales of the best wines in Europe, which have never been accurately defined and classified for a world market. In other words, a wine bluffer can conduct his own research into such unknown and unclassified wines.

As it is, most of the wines exported from the continents of Africa,

America and Australia are shipped to France or Germany and are used for blending into unidentifiable everyday wines sold under some brand name, if the appellation laws are not actually being broken. It is alarming to think that a bottle of 'Beaujolais' may be half full of a red wine from Chile, or a 'Liebfraumilch' may be pressed from Australian Riesling grapes. With the increasing world demand for wine, it behoves the authorities of countries relatively new at producing wine to do all they can to improve quality and marketing methods: a population explosion of wine drinkers will exhaust European stocks, and more decent wine has got to come from somewhere.

Other European Wines
Hungary
Produces a coarse red wine which sells best on its name: bull's blood. But one of the great wines of the world was 'Imperial Tokay', no longer – surprisingly – produced under a Communist regime. Reported by the medical profession to be an effective restorer of virility and increaser of fertility, there was a considerable demand for this white wine in the days of the Hapsburg Austro-Hungarian Empire. Heigh ho for Ruritania. There is a golden wine produced today from the vineyards; but however good and rich, it can't be the same.

Yugoslavia
Exports some pleasant white wines produced in Dalmatia – normally called 'Sylvaner' or other grape names – often from the district of Lutomer.

Switzerland
Produces a small amount of wine, the best of which is white and fruity. Like the country, the wine is reliable, not desperately inspiring and rather too expensive. The best comes from the Valais, the Vaud, and Neuchatel districts.

Greece
Is responsible for producing a disgusting resin-flavoured stuff called Retsina, a sweet wine from Samos, and rather horrid food. Until they do something to improve the standards of gastronomy – and, incidentally, of government, they do not deserve recognition, even if they have got very beautiful remains and islands.

A totally useless Glossary to bluff People with

Acetic Acid	Acid responsible for the vinegar taste in an 'off' wine.
Aigre	The sourness caused by the acetic acid.
Aligoté	Grape used for making a light white wine in Burgundy. The wine is often named after it. e.g. Bourgogne Aligoté.
Amertume	Bitterness, often called greenness due to the fact that the wine is young or is possibly suffering from travel sickness. It can also be 'over the top'.
Apré	Harsh.
Appellation Contrôlée	A term indicating that the wine conforms to certain geographical and qualitative requirements laid down by the French Government.
Body	A term describing the fullness of a wine; a quality made by the combination of alcohol and fruit.
Bottle Sickness	A temporary ailment found in a wine for a short time after it has been bottled.
Bouchonné	A wine that has been contaminated by a faulty cork.
Bouquet	The smell or fragrance of a wine. One of its greatest properties.
Brut	Unsweetened or very dry. Often used in Champagne.
Cabernet Franc	The great grape of the Médoc. Used for making the best red wines.
Capsule	A cap which protects the exposed surface of a cork. In certain German vineyards its colour is used to denote the quality of the wine. e.g. Schloss Vollrads.
Cassis	A Provence wine. Also a blackcurrant liqueur and cordial.

Cellier	Wine vault or store.
Cépage	A species of wine. e.g. Pinot Noir, Riesling.
Chai	An above-ground store for wine. c.f. cellier.
Chambrer	A French term meaning to bring to room temperature. NOT to warm.
Chaptalisation	A strictly controlled practice by which sugar, which will be fermented into alcohol and thereby raise the alcoholic strength, is added. (After Jean Antoine Chaptal 1756–1832.)
Château	Either a castle or, particularly in Bordeaux, the building in which the wine is made. Many of the 'Châteaux' in Bordeaux are far from being castles.
Château-Bottled	This, on a label, means that the wine was bottled where it was made. It is written in French either as 'Mise en bouteille au Château' or 'Mise au Château'.
Chenin Blanc	A species of grape found chiefly in the Loire area Used for making quality white wines.
Clairet	French name for a light red wine. The word 'claret' is thought to have derived from this word.
Climat	A Burgundian word given to certain vineyards. Means growth or 'cru'.
Clos	French for enclosure. Refers to an enclosed vineyard. e.g. Clos de Vougeot.
Commune	Parish.
Corked	English translation of Bouchonné.
Corsé	A rather 'larger than life' wine. The bigger body and elevated alcoholic content, however, remain in balance.
Coupage	The practice of blending wine.
Coupé	Blended.
Cramant	A village on the Cote des Blancs, which produce some of the finest white grapes used in the making of Champagne.

Cru	Means growth. Used to indicate a certain vineyard or group of vineyards which produce wines of the same standard and quality.
Cru Bourgeois	A wine, of medium standard, made from grapes of unclassified growths.
Cuve	Means vat.
Cuvée	Vatting. Refers to the blending of wines from different vineyards but the same vintage.
Dégorger	The process in champagne-making in which the sediment in the bottle is removed with a minimum loss of gas and wine.
Demi-sec	Definitely on the sweet side of medium.
Depôt	Deposit.
Domaine	Property. The Burgundian equivalent of Château.
Doux	Sweet. In Champagne it means a very sweet wine.
Dur	Hard. 'Green'. Usually owing to the raised tannin level, common to young wines.
Égrappées	Grapes which have been separated from their stalks.
Égrappoir	The machine which separates the grapes from the stalks. It consists, in principle, of a rotating callender barrel.
Espumoso	Spanish for sparkling.
Fermé	Slightly hard.
Fermentation	The essential process of wine making whereby the grape sugar is converted to alcohol.
Feuillette	Half a hogshead.
Foudres	Large capacity vats in which blending is carried out.
Frais	Chilled.
Frappé	Iced.
Fruité	Fruity, usually owing to the presence of unfermented grape sugar.

Fuder	A cask of 960 litres used in the Moselle and Palatinate area of Germany.
Gamay	A species of grape which produces very large quantities of red wine which, although never great, is often good. The Beaujolais, Chalonnais, and Maconnais areas are planted out in this grape.
Goût	Taste
Goût de Bouchon	Same as Bouchonné.
Goût de Terroir	The taste imparted to the wine by the soil in which the vine was grown.
Grande Marque	Term denoting a first class champagne.
Growth	Same as 'cru'.
Hectare	A French measure of area which is equivalent to 2.47 acres.
Hectolitre	A French measure of volume which is equal to 100 litres or 22 Imp. gals.
Hogshead	A wooden cask of 46–48 gals. capacity.
Ice Wines	Wines made in Germany from grapes picked so late that ice has formed on them. In general, these wines are very good indeed.
Imperial	A bottle of 8 ordinary bottles capacity.
Jeroboam	A bottle of 4 ordinary bottles capacity.
Keller	German for cellar.
Liqueur de tirage	A solution, used in champagne making at the time of the first bottling. It is made up of cane sugar dissolved in champagne.
Madérisé	A term used to indicate that a white wine has aged and become oxidised. This is reflected in the wine acquiring a brownish colour.
Magnum	A bottle which has the capacity of two ordinary bottles.
Marc	A liqueur made from distilling the last pressings of grapes, or any other fruit, which needs several years ageing before it loses its hardness and becomes soft and palatable.

Merlot	One of the noble grapes of Bordeaux, used in the making of some of the great red wines.
Methuselah	A bottle of Champagne with the capacity of 8 ordinary bottles. It is very rare.
Millésime	The date of the vintage.
Millésimé	A dated or vintage wine.
Moelleux	Soft and smooth.
Montilla	A dry wine made outside the official sherry growing area in Spain. Drunk like sherry.
Mousseux	Sparkling.
Moût	Must. The unfermented grape juice.
Mùr	Ripe.
Muté	A wine, in which the fermentation has been arrested by the addition of spirit.
Natur, Naturrein, Naturwein	German term meaning that a wine has been fermented without the addition of sugar.
Nature	In France, a term applied specifically to champagne, showing that it is unsweetened.
Non-vintage	A wine made from wines of different vintages.
Nose	Bouquet.
Oenology	The Science of wine-making.
Oidium	One of the most common of wine diseases; from a fungus.
Ordinaire	Plain. Undistinguished.
Passe-Tous-Grains	A Burgundian wine up from a mixture of Pinot and Gamay grapes.
Pasteurisé	A wine treated by heat to kill all ferments.
Pays, Vin de	Peasant wine, usually ordinaire.
Pelure d'Oignon	The colour of onion skin which is applied to certain rosé wines.
Pétillant	A slightly sparkling wine, owing to the presence of a small amount of carbon dioxide gas.

Phylloxera	A terrible scourge caused by a burrowing louse which attacks the vine-root. It came to Europe in about 1870 and destroyed most of the vineyards, which are now planted out with American roots which are resistant to the louse.
Pièce	A hogshead, containing about 225 litres.
Pinot Blanc or Chardonnay	A white grape grown in Burgundy and Champagne. It is responsible for the finest wines from those districts.
Pinot Noir or Noirien	A black grape which produces the great red wine for Burgundy and goes into the making of the finest champagnes.
Piqué	A wine which has become, or is becoming, vinegary.
Pourriture Noble	A form of mould which is purposely allowed to form on the grapes in certain areas which make sweet wines. In particular in the Sauterne district, and in parts of Germany which produce auslesen wines.
Premier Cru	Literally means 'first growth'. Refers to the finest wines.
Pressoir	The apparatus used for pressing the grapes.
Punt	The hollow found in the bottom of certain bottles.
Quart de Chaume	An excellent Loire wine, coming from the Coteaux du Layon.
Race	Breed.
Rehoboam	A bottle having the capacity of 6 ordinary bottles; rarely found except occasionally in champagne.
Robe	The colour of a wine.
Rosé	A pink wine.
Saint Émilion	This red wine from Bordeaux has a darker colour than most Médoc wines, but does not last as long.

Sauvignon Blanc	One of the most noble of the white grapes. Used for Pouilly Blanc Fumé and also in Sauternes, where it is mixed with Semillon to produce some of the greatest white wines in the world.
Sec	Means dry. Often used to indicate the degree of dryness which can, paradoxically, sometimes be sweet. e.g. demi-sec.
Sekt	German for sparkling wine.
Sémillon	The species of grape responsible for the finest white wines of Bordeaux. (see Sauvignon) It is also planted elsewhere.
Sommelier	The wine butler.
Souche	The root stock.
Soutirage	Racking, which is a process whereby the wine is separated from its impurities. It is carried out about three times during the development of the wine.
Spritzig	The German word for 'pétillant'.
Spumante	The Italian for 'sparkling'.
Sylvaner	A species of grape which is the Gamay of Germany. That is, it is used more for the quantity of wine produced, than its quality. It is found in Alsace, Germany, and Austria; the wine is white.
Syrah	A species of noble, black grape which is found in the Rhône valley, in particular.
Tannin	A very important ingredient in the skin of black grapes which plays an indispensable role in the ageing process of a wine. It has a bitter hard taste, easily recognised in young wines.
Tendre	Light and agreeable wine, although unlikely to last very long.
Tête de Cuvée	In Sauternes, the first drawing off of the wine. In Burgundy the phrase refers to the best wine from a certain vineyard.
Tirage	Bottling.

Tonneau	A French cask which has a capacity of four hogsheads. Rarely seen nowadays.
Valinch	An outsize pipette which is used for taking samples out of a cask of wine.
V.D.Q.S.	'Vin Délimité de Qualité Superieure.' An official wine standard between vin ordinaire and those having an 'appelation contrôlée.'
Velours	Velvet. A particularly soft wine.
Vendange	The grape harvest.
Venencia	The Spanish word for Valinch.
Verzy	A village which produces fine grapes for making champagne.
Vigneron	A grower of vines.
Vignoble	French for vineyard.
Vin	French for wine.
Vin de Consommation Courante, Vin Ordinaire	A wine for everyday drinking.
Vintage	Means either the gathering of the grapes or, if followed by a year, that the wine was made from grapes only harvested in that year.
Yeast	A fungus which gathers as a 'dust' on the skins of the grapes. It is an indispensable agent during the fermentation of the must.
Zwicker	Indicates that a wine has been made from blending different grapes. It is used in Alsace.

Know Your Vintages

Year	Port	Claret	Burgundy	Rhone	Rhine Moselle	Sauterne	White Burgundy	Champagne
1945	7	6	7	6	6	7	6	6
1946	5	3	4	4	4	3	5	3
1947	7	7	7	7	6	7	7	7
1948	7	6	5	4	5	4	5	4
1949	4	7	6	6	5	5	6	6
1950	6	5	4	6	7	4	6	6
1951	3	3	3	4	5	3	3	3
1952	4	6	7	7	2	6	6	2
1953	4	7	6	6	6	7	7	7
1954	5	4	4	5	7	3	4	7
1955	7	6	6	7	3	6	6	7
1956	2	3	2	5	5	3	3	3
1957	5	5	5	5	3	4	5	7
1958	5	5	4	4	5	3	3	4
1959	3	7	6	6	5	5	5	2
1960	7	4	5	6	7	7	4	5
1961	4	7	6	5	5	4	7	6
1962	5	6	6	5	5	5	3	4
1963	6	4	4	5	6	6	7	7
1964	4	6	6	7	4	2	5	6
1965	6	4	4	5	6	3	6	4
1966	5	6	4	6	3	3	4	7
								5
								6

0 = NO GOOD   7 = THE BEST

We are indebted for this chart to The Wine and Food Society, who prepared it for the benefit of its members, and of others interested in good wine. Every care has been taken to make it an accurate index of fact at the time of its publication: nevertheless it must be remembered that there are exceptions to all rules: there are always some very good wines made when a vintage is not deserving of the highest marks, just as there are, unfortunately, some bad wines made in the best vintages. A good wine merchant will advise you.